I0808998
THROUGH THE DECADES
THE 1980S
The Color Purple
Alice Walker
FEED THE WORLD
eureka!
BY ALICIA Z. KLEPEIS

Eureka! books turn real stories into unforgettable experiences. This nonfiction imprint sparks curiosity, encourages critical thinking, and engages middle-grade readers. *Eureka!* books empower young minds to explore the stories of the real world, one fascinating fact at a time. Unravel the power of knowledge and lifelong learning with *Eureka!*

This edition first published in 2026 by Bellwether Media, Inc.

Library of Congress Cataloging-in-Publication Data

LC record for The 1980s available at: https://lccn.loc.gov/2025024351

Editor: Christina Leaf Series Designer: Andrea Schneider Book Designer: Laura Sowers

Printed in the United States of America, North Mankato, MN.

TABLE OF CONTENTS

WELCOME TO THE 1980s!

After school, a kid is walking to a friend's house. She pulls her Walkman out of her backpack and slips in a Madonna cassette. The girl stops briefly at a convenience store. She buys a box of Nerds and a pack of Hawaiian Punch juice boxes.

When she arrives at her friend's house, they make some microwave popcorn. They watch a little MTV before checking out ABC Afterschool Specials. When it is over, they throw on their Reebok sneakers and head outside. They soon join a neighborhood game of capture of the flag.

After the game, the girl heads home for dinner. It is her favorite, Hamburger Helper. She plays *Pac-Man* and *Space Invaders* with her family on their old Atari 2600 gaming system after dinner. Then, she reads the September 1986 issue of *YM* magazine before bed. She loves the article about movie star Tom Cruise. It was a great day for this '80s kid!

Listening to Cassettes

WHAT HAPPENED IN THE 1980s?

In contrast to previous decades, the 1980s was a period more focused on prosperity than protests. Many Americans devoted their energy to achieving material wealth and success. President Ronald Reagan led the United States with a sense of optimism and national pride. His administration emphasized the importance of big business and a strong military.

Not all Americans benefited from Reagan's policies. Cuts in government-funded social services left many people struggling. The economic policies known as **Reaganomics** saw the poor get poorer, particularly Black, Latino, and Native American populations. Yet, women made big strides in closing the wage gap between men and women during this decade.

Technological innovation boomed all decade long. Computers became more sophisticated and more accessible to average people. Space travel and medical technology also improved greatly.

Throughout the 1980s, political conflict and violence plagued nations around the world. Longstanding rifts brought death and destruction to some Middle Eastern and Asian nations, including Iraq, Iran, and Afghanistan. However, new **labor unions** and political parties brought change to peoples' lives in parts of Europe.

HOW MUCH?

1 GALLON GAS

$1.19 (1980)
$1.00 (1989)

THE NEW YORK TIMES

(weekday issue)

$0.25 (1980) | $0.40 (1989)

MOVIE TICKET

$2.69 (1980)
$3.99 (1989)

FIRST-CLASS STAMP

$0.15 (1980)
$0.25 (1989)

LOAF OF BREAD

$0.50 (1981)
$0.67 (1989)

1 GALLON MILK

$1.12 (1980)
$1.17 (1989)

A DOZEN EGGS

$0.88 (1980)
$1.08 (1989)

HERSHEY BAR

$0.25 (1980)
$0.40 (1986)

HISTORY

UNITED STATES HISTORY

When the 1980s began, the **Cold War** still dominated America's foreign policy. President Reagan viewed **communism** as a threat to freedom around the world. He introduced the Reagan Doctrine, which provided military and financial support to groups fighting against communism. This caused U.S. military spending to skyrocket.

The Iran-Contra Affair was a complex political scandal during this decade. It involved the secret sale of weapons to Iran in exchange for the release of American hostages. Some of the profits made from these sales went toward illegally funding the Contras, a rebel group in Nicaragua.

Economic challenges pushed the Federal Reserve Chairman to work to reduce **inflation**, in part through tax cuts and reduced government spending. Varying unemployment rates made it hard for many Americans to thrive. But the wealthy grew richer, driving a greater wealth gap amongst Americans.

PRESIDENT RONALD REAGAN

IRAN-CONTRA AFFAIR PRESS CONFERENCE

PROTESTING INFLATION

MOUNT SAINT HELENS

On May 18, 1980, Washington State experienced the volcanic eruption of Mount Saint Helens. This eruption caused a landslide and the deaths of 57 people. It also leveled homes and trees in the surrounding area.

EXXON VALDEZ

On March 24, 1989, the *Exxon Valdez* oil tanker ran aground in Alaska. Eleven million gallons of oil spilled into Prince William Sound. It was one of the biggest environmental disasters in American history. Hundreds of thousands of animals died and the surrounding habitats were devastated.

THE DISARMAMENT MOVEMENT

Despite increased military involvement around the world, progress was made in the disarmament movement. On June 12, 1982, about a million people gathered in New York City's Central Park to protest nuclear weapons. In December 1987, Soviet leader Mikhail Gorbachev made a historic visit to the U.S. During this visit, Reagan and Gorbachev signed the Intermediate-Range Nuclear Forces Treaty. It eliminated a whole class of nuclear weapons.

UNITED STATES POLITICS

The **conservative** agendas of many political leaders of the 1980s contrasted with those of **liberal** 1970s leaders like Jimmy Carter. President Reagan's economic policy gave tax cuts to businesses and the wealthy. Politicians believed this would boost spending, and savings would trickle down to lower classes. But the policy was largely unsuccessful.

President Ronald Reagan

ELECTION SHOWDOWN:
1980 PRESIDENTIAL ELECTION

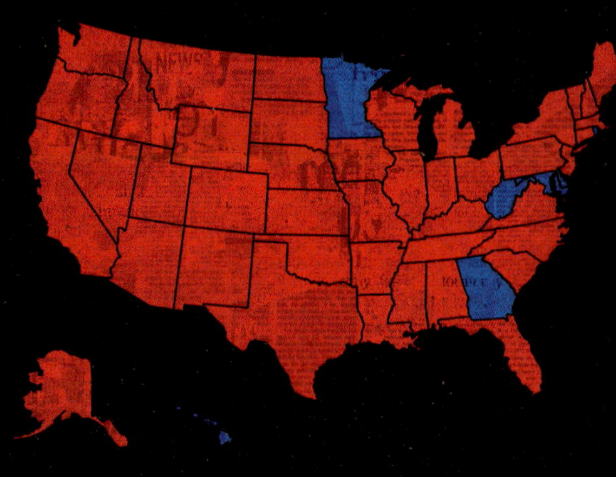

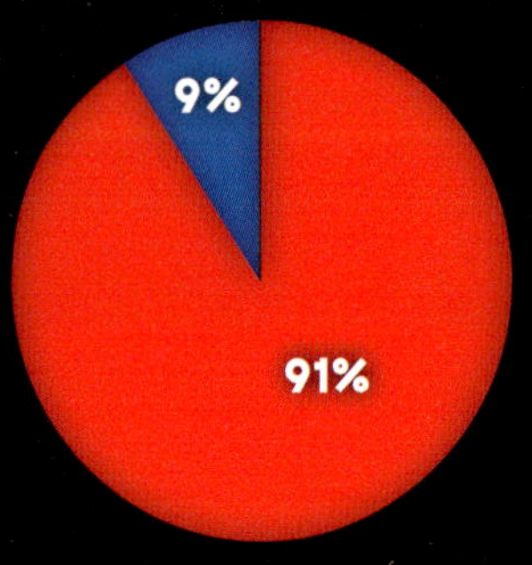

The Reagan administration also worked to roll back many of the environmental policies from the 1960s and 1970s. It dramatically cut funding and staff to agencies like the Environmental Protection Agency (EPA). For example, the EPA's science budget was cut by 58 percent between 1980 and 1983, greatly reducing its ability to carry out research.

American politics saw women blaze new paths in several roles during the decade. In 1981, Sandra Day O'Connor became the first woman to serve on the U.S. Supreme Court. Three years later, Democrat Geraldine Ferraro was the first female vice presidential candidate on a major party ticket.

Despite the conservatism, progress was made on some liberal agendas. The **LGBTQ+** community saw some movement forward in 1982. That year, Wisconsin became the first state to ban **discrimination** against people based on their sexual orientation.

SWEARING IN OF SANDRA DAY O'CONNOR

GERALDINE FERRARO

PEOPLE PROTESTING FOR LGBTQ+ RIGHTS

MAINE INDIAN CLAIMS SETTLEMENT ACT

In October 1980, President Carter signed the Maine Indian Claims Settlement Act. It granted $81.5 million to Native American tribes including the Maliseet, Passamaquoddy, and Penobscot as payment for land taken from them.

SPOTLIGHT ON:

THE AIDS CRISIS

In 1981, doctors in Los Angeles and New York City reported on a mysterious new disease. Some of the first patients had a rare form of cancer. Others had a rare form of pneumonia. These illnesses showed that patients had a weakened **immune system**. All of these initial patients were gay men.

There was a **stigma** associated with this new disease. Part of this was due to fear and the lack of knowledge about how it spread. But it was also stigmatized because it was seen as a "gay" disease. This may be why the government initially offered little help in studying the disease.

In 1982, the Centers for Disease Control and Prevention (CDC) gave a new name to the disease: AIDS. It stands for acquired immunodeficiency syndrome. Researchers learned that AIDS is caused by the HIV virus. The virus is spread through blood and some other bodily fluids. By 1986, AIDS cases had been reported in 85 nations. In addition to gay men, patients included straight men, women, and children.

A major breakthrough happened in 1987. The FDA approved AZT, the first anti-HIV medication. **Advocacy** groups worked to provide people with more information about how to stop the spread of AIDS. In 1988, every U.S. household received a brochure titled "Understanding AIDS." Despite eventual advocacy, the disease killed around 100,000 Americans during the decade.

MAKING HEADLINES

"A Disease's Spread Provokes Anxiety"

—*The New York Times*, August 8, 1982

"AIDS HELP 'TOO LATE FOR VICTIMS'"

—*THE GUARDIAN*, APRIL 25, 1984

AZT

WHO'S WHO?

MICHAEL GOTTLIEB

ROLE:
Doctor who made the first clinical description of AIDS

KNOWN FOR:
The doctor who worked with some of the first patients displaying the failing immune systems typical of AIDS victims and published the June 5, 1981, report that marks the beginning of the AIDS epidemic

ROCK HUDSON

ROLE:
Brought attention to the AIDS epidemic

KNOWN FOR:
An actor known for his good looks and charisma whose death from AIDS brought attention to the AIDS epidemic and led many people to raise money for AIDS research

WORLD HISTORY

International conflicts and major regime changes marked the 1980s. Iraqi forces invaded Iran in 1980. This led to an eight-year-long war that claimed the lives of more than one million people. As the war continued, 52 American hostages were released from Iran in January 1981 after 444 days in captivity. Soviet forces fought against anti-communist rebels in Afghanistan throughout the decade. This war, combined with the arms race with the U.S., negatively impacted the already struggling Soviet economy.

Mikhail Gorbachev took over power of the Soviet Union in 1985. He aimed to both restructure the Soviet economy and improve relations with the U.S. His new policies of reconstruction and openness offered hope of future freedom for Soviet citizens.

Several new countries were established during the 1980s. Zimbabwe is in Africa. Belize is in Central America. Caribbean island countries include Antigua and Barbuda and Saint Kitts and Nevis. Vanuatu, Brunei, the Marshall Islands, and the Federated States of Micronesia are in the Pacific Ocean.

RETURN OF AMERICAN HOSTAGES

MIKHAIL GORBACHEV

BELIZE INDEPENDENCE DAY, 1981

TIANANMEN SQUARE

The 1980s were a time of major changes for China. The economy had grown remarkably. More Chinese people were exposed to new ideas and improved standards of living. Despite the changes, there was still unrest. Students led protests beginning in the mid-1980s. They demanded greater political freedom. In June 1989, pro-democratic protests in Beijing's Tiananmen Square were crushed by Chinese armed forces.

Tiananmen Square protest

WEDDING OF THE CENTURY

On July 29, 1981, Britain's Prince Charles and Lady Diana Spencer were married in what was described as "the wedding of the century." Hundreds of thousands of spectators lined London's streets to celebrate. About 750 million people in 74 nations watched the elaborate ceremony on television.

THE FALL OF THE BERLIN WALL

After World War II, Germany was split into two countries. East Germany was controlled by the Soviet Union. West Germany aligned with the U.S. and its allies. East and West Germany were divided by the Berlin Wall in 1961. The wall became a symbol of the Cold War. Political changes and civil unrest led to the wall's dismantling in November 1989. Germany became a reunited nation in October 1990.

Berlin Wall

SPOTLIGHT ON:

CHERNOBYL

On April 26, 1986, an industrial disaster occurred at the Chernobyl **nuclear power plant** in Ukraine. During a test, workers lost control of one of the plant's reactors. This caused two explosions and a fire that destroyed the building housing the reactor. Huge amounts of toxic **radiation** went into the atmosphere. The wind spread radioactive material as far as Sweden.

Pripyat, a town just 1.9 miles (3 kilometers) from the plant, was totally evacuated after the accident. Around 350,000 people are thought to have been relocated in total. Two plant workers were killed by the initial explosion. Another 28 firefighters and emergency cleanup crew members died within three months from acute radiation sickness. Contamination spread across much of Europe, causing an increase in cancer in the more immediate area for many years after the accident.

After the accident, it became clear that plant workers had made errors, and proper safety protocols were not in place. The accident gave a major push to the anti-nuclear movement around the world. The disaster's economic and political costs sped up the decline of the Soviet Union.

MAKING HEADLINES

"Soviet Announces Nuclear Accident at Electric Plant"

—*The New York Times*, April 29, 1986

CHERNOBYL POWER PLANT AFTER THE ACCIDENT

"RADIOACTIVE RUSSIAN DUST CLOUD ESCAPES"

—*THE GUARDIAN*, APRIL 29, 1986

"Soviet Reactor Fails, Spews Radioactivity"

—*The San Diego Union*, April 29, 1986

WHO'S WHO?

VIKTOR BRYUKHANOV

ROLE:

Director and engineer at Chernobyl Nuclear Power Plant

KNOWN FOR:

A highly trained administrator of the plant since 1970, Bryukhanov approved the launch of Reactor Number 4 despite missing a required safety test. He was later convicted for violating safety regulations that led to the accident.

SOCIAL CHANGES

The 1980s saw some significant changes in the structure of many U.S. households. For the first time in history, more than one out of four were nonfamily households. Individuals living alone made up most of these. More non-married couples also lived together during the 1980s than in previous decades.

Interracial marriage became more common among all racial and educational groups. The approval of interracial marriages increased significantly, creating a positive shift in race relations.

More Americans earned college degrees in the 1980s than ever before. By this decade, the majority of undergraduates across the U.S were women. Perhaps as a result, women working in management positions increased significantly. Most of these new women managers were white women, although women of color in management also saw their numbers increase.

Despite educational advances and some workplace changes, many Americans did not see improvements in their daily lives. In fact, difficult economic conditions and cuts to housing assistance programs led to a huge surge in the number of unhoused Americans. These included veterans, people with mental illnesses, and individuals with AIDS, among others.

INTERRACIAL MARRIAGE

KATHARINE GRAHAM, PUBLISHER OF *THE WASHINGTON POST*, 1963 TO 1991

PROTESTING HOUSELESSNESS

Prime Minister Benazir Bhutto

POLITICAL TRAILBLAZERS

In 1980, Finland's Vigdís Finnbogadóttir became the first woman to be democratically elected as the president of a country. Benazir Bhutto became the prime minister of Pakistan in 1988. She was the first female leader of a Muslim country in modern history. Dominica, Norway, Malta, and the Philippines also had their first women leaders.

SCIENCE AND TECHNOLOGY

TECHNOLOGICAL ADVANCEMENTS

The 1980s was critical to the development and availability of many technologies people now use in their daily lives. Today, nearly all U.S. households have at least one cell phone. But it was not until 1983 that mobile phones became commercially available. That year, Motorola launched the DynaTAC 8000X. It weighed a little less than 2 pounds (1 kilogram) and cost $3,995. That was more than $12,000 in today's money!

The invention of camcorders in the early 1980s gave people the chance to make better quality home videos than ever before. Disposable cameras, or single-use cameras, came out in the mid-1980s. Photographers enjoyed these inexpensive, lightweight, and easy-to-use cameras.

MICROSOFT WINDOWS 1.0

WHAT IS IT:
An operating system for personal computers

INVENTOR:
Bill Gates

YEAR INVENTED:
1985

EFFECT ON DAILY LIFE:
Made personal computers more user friendly

Advances in personal computers, such as faster **microprocessors** and additional memory, soared over the course of the decade. This led to more people having them at home. The first Apple Macintosh went on sale in 1984. Its graphical user interface made it easier for people to start using computers. Instead of having to write commands to tell the computer what to do, visual elements like icons and windows helped users do tasks intuitively. User-friendly systems like these made using a mouse with a computer standard in the 1980s. The Microsoft Windows operating system was released in 1985. It remains the world's most popular operating system for desktops and laptops.

TIME "PERSON" OF THE YEAR

TIME **magazine has named a Person of The Year since 1927. In 1982, the award was changed to "Machine of the Year" when it was given to the personal computer.**

camcorder

SCIENTIFIC AND MEDICAL ADVANCEMENTS

The 1980s was a time of amazing scientific advances. NASA launched its first space shuttle, Columbia, on April 12, 1981. This was the first spacecraft that could be reused. NASA's space shuttle program was essential to constructing the International Space Station in the 1990s and 2000s.

In 1983, Sally Ride became the first American woman to go into space. She traveled aboard the space shuttle Challenger. Unfortunately, a mechanical failure caused Challenger to be torn apart in midair in January 1986. All seven crew members were killed.

The first hepatitis B vaccine was approved for use in 1981. Because hepatitis B is a cause of liver cancer, the vaccine is often described as "the first anti-cancer vaccine." Surgical techniques improved greatly in the 1980s. William DeVries performed the first successful permanent artificial heart transplant in 1982. In 1985, a surgical robotic arm called PUMA 560 was used during a brain biopsy procedure.

Scientists announced a hole in Earth's **ozone layer** in 1985. This discovery led to a huge push in both **climate change** research and the environmental movement.

SALLY RIDE

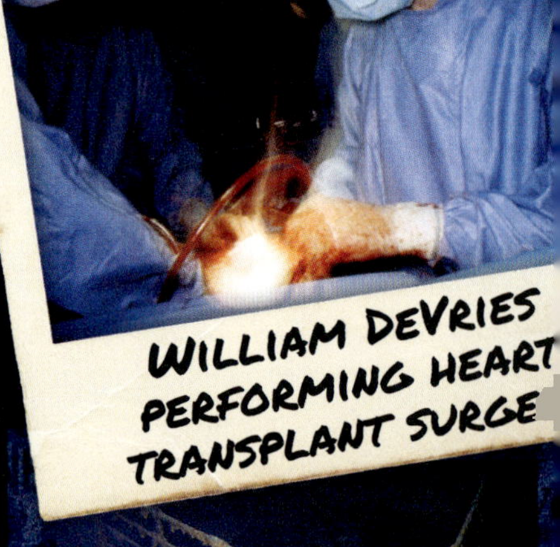

WILLIAM DEVRIES PERFORMING HEART TRANSPLANT SURGE

TITANIC DISCOVERY

Oceanographer Robert Ballard and his team discovered the wreckage of the RMS *Titanic* on September 1, 1985. It was found around 400 miles (644 kilometers) off the Canadian coast at a depth of roughly 12,600 feet (3,840 meters).

launch of the Space Shuttle Columbia

DAILY LIFE

LIFE IN THE '80s

Family structures continued to change during the 1980s. Divorce rates were high, leading to more single-parent families. A desire for more **disposable income** meant that, in many other families, both parents worked. These factors led to a greater demand for daycare. But some children were left unsupervised after school until their parents came home. They were known as "latchkey kids."

By the end of the 1980s, more Americans lived in urban areas than ever before. While some areas of cities became **gentrified** during the decade, city dwellers with enough money commonly moved to suburban areas.

Early 1980s families often used station wagons to get around. But the first minivans hit the U.S. market in 1983. Their popularity soared during the decade. Teens often asked for rides to the mall where they could shop, hang out with friends, or visit a video game arcade. The Home Shopping Network and QVC made shopping via TV possible. Both started broadcasting in the 1980s.

MINIVAN

VIDEO GAME ARCADE

EPCOT

Located in Walt Disney World, the EPCOT theme park opened on October 1, 1982. A day pass for teens cost just $15!

1980s SLANG

BUFF
very muscular

book it
to move quickly

VEG OUT
to relax

RALPH
to throw up

gnarly
awesome or dangerous or disgusting

BOGUS
ridiculous or fake

Totally tubular
awesome

take a chill pill!
Relax!

Fresh
new or exciting

FASHION TRENDS

In many ways, 1980s fashion favored **maximalism** and contrast. The style of young urban professionals, also known as "yuppies," showed off their status and success. Men often wore pinstripe business suits known as power suits. As more women climbed the corporate ladder, they too wore power suits that typically featured pencil skirts. Big shoulder pads were common in jackets for both sexes.

The preppy look was a conservative trend. Polo shirts, shoulder-draped sweaters, khakis, and plaid shorts were celebrated preppy fashion choices.

British punk trends of the 1970s influenced widespread punk looks in the 1980s. Edgy clothing included safety-pin-studded ripped jeans, band T-shirts, and leather jackets. Doc Martens combat boots were all the rage. Brightly dyed hair and wild styles including mohawks were also major elements of the punk look.

everyday athletic wear

Everyday athletic wear was another new trend. People sported tracksuits, usually in bold or neon colors. Stirrup pants were often paired with legwarmers. Lycra and spandex, both stretchy fabrics, appeared in clothing from workout wear to formfitting bodycon dresses.

When it came to hairstyles, bigger was better in the 1980s. Curly hair was in. Those not born with it often went to the salon to get permanent waves, or perms. Celebrities from tennis star Andre Agassi to actor Patrick Swayze wore mullets.

POWER SUITS

PUNK FASHION

Andre Agassi with a mullet

JELLY SHOES

Jelly shoes were a fashionable footwear in the 1980s. Made of flexible PVC plastic, they came in many colors and styles. At first, they appeared in high-end department stores. Designers like Jean Paul Gaultier made "jellies" worn by celebrities such as Madonna. But they soon became the inexpensive, colorful "it" shoe that appealed to kids and adults alike.

PRODUCTS AND TOYS

Video game consoles and electronic toys grew in popularity throughout the 1980s. But many of the decade's most iconic and well-loved toys did not need power sources or batteries. From stuffed animals to dolls to arts and crafts, '80s kids had many entertainment options!

PAC-MAN

One of the best-known video games of all time, *Pac-Man* debuted in Tokyo, Japan, on May 22, 1980. This maze game quickly spread to arcades and video game consoles in homes around the world. It inspired the creation of *Ms. Pac-Man* in 1982.

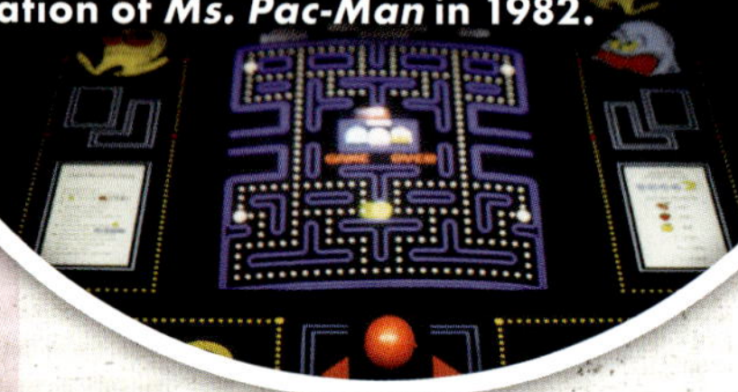

RUBIK'S CUBE

Invented by Hungarian design teacher Ernő Rubik, this plastic puzzle came out in stores in 1980. Players tried to get the cube's six sides to be the same color. The Rubik's Cube quickly became "the best-selling puzzle toy in history."

TRIVIAL PURSUIT

First launched in 1981, Trivial Pursuit was one of the decade's best-loved board games. Its first version offered trivia buffs 6,000 questions. It featured categories including geography, entertainment, sports, and history. The original has led to many spinoffs.

SHRINKY DINKS

Although invented in 1973, the popularity of Shrinky Dinks peaked during the 1980s. It involved coloring thin sheets of a plastic called polystyrene and cutting them into various shapes. The cutouts would then bake in an oven where they would shrink and thicken.

KOOSH BALL

The Koosh Ball was first introduced in 1987. The idea came when creator Scott Stillinger was trying to teach his children to catch. The wriggly ball is made up of many individual rubber fibers, making it easy to grip. The ball was named after the sound it makes when it is caught.

CABBAGE PATCH KIDS

Cabbage Patch Kids made their debut in 1983. That holiday season, demand for these dolls boomed. Shoppers had trouble finding them! The soft-bodied dolls had unique names and features, such as dimples, different-colored eyes, and hair. They came with adoption papers and a birth certificate.

TRANSFORMERS ACTION FIGURES

Hasbro debuted the first Transformers action figures in 1984. *The Transformers* animated TV series and comics to go along with the toys were released soon after. Each toy robot could change into another form, whether a vehicle, object, or animal. The Autobot Commander Optimus Prime was an essential collectible from the series.

POUND PUPPIES

Pound Puppies were stuffed animals released in 1984. Children were drawn to these cuddly pooches who came packaged in a cardboard carrier. They soon became the subject of a popular animated TV series.

TEDDY RUXPIN

Teddy Ruxpin was an electronic plush toy that first came out in 1985. Once a cassette was inserted into its back, this **animatronic** bear could "read" stories. Teddy Ruxpin's eyes blinked and mouth moved while it told stories. This toy was a huge seller!

ARTS AND ENTERTAINMENT

PUBLICATIONS

The 1980s had something for every reader. *Cosmos* by Carl Sagan and *A Brief History of Time* by Stephen Hawking were two of the most popular nonfiction books. These books made complex scientific topics more approachable. Science fiction, especially dystopian works like *The Handmaid's Tale* and *Ender's Game*, was big in the decade.

Much of the decade's celebrated literature focused on the experiences of **marginalized** people. Two Black writers won Pulitzer Prizes for fiction during the 1980s. Toni Morrison won for *Beloved*, and Alice Walker won for *The Color Purple*. Lois Lowry's 1989 novel, *Number the Stars*, won the Newbery Medal. It tells of a young girl's family trying to help Jewish friends escape the Nazis during World War II.

Magazines continued to specialize throughout the 1980s. They targeted readers with different hobbies, food preferences, and more.

READING REC

TITLE:
HATCHET

AUTHOR:
Gary Paulsen

YEAR PUBLISHED:
1987

SUMMARY:
Brian, a 13-year-old boy, is stranded in the Canadian wilderness following a plane crash. This amazing story follows Brian as he struggles to survive and shares the discoveries he makes along the way.

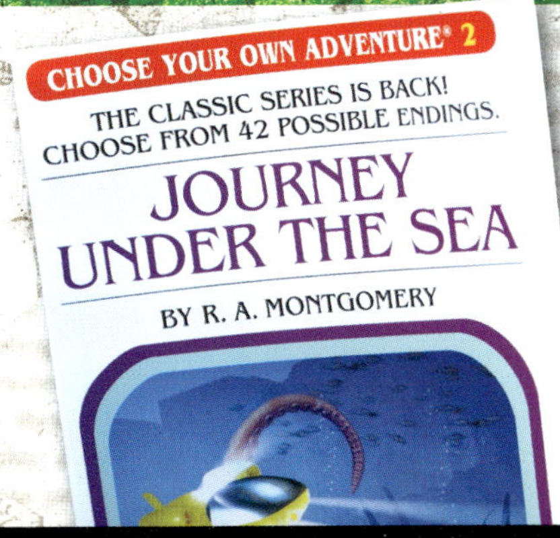

CHOOSE YOUR OWN ADVENTURE

Choose Your Own Adventure was one of the most popular series of the 1980s. These unique gamebooks allowed readers to be the protagonist by making choices that determined what happened next. The protagonist could be a spy, mountain climber, or even a race car driver. Over 250 million copies were sold between 1979 and 1999.

CHRIS VAN ALLSBURG

The works of author-illustrator Chris Van Allsburg are known for their combination of fantasy and reality. His book *Jumanji*, released in 1981, and the 1985 title *The Polar Express* won Caldecott Medals. Both books were later made into successful movies.

THE HOUSE ON MANGO STREET

Sandra Cisneros's novel *The House on Mango Street* came out in 1984. It tells the story of Esperanza, a Mexican-American girl growing up in Chicago. The book addresses issues such as puberty, poverty, and racism. It is now an important part of many middle and high school reading curriculums.

BEVERLY CLEARY

Already a well-established author, Beverly Cleary's superstar status grew in the 1980s. She won the National Book Award in 1981 for *Ramona and Her Mother*. Her 1984 novel *Dear Mr. Henshaw* won that year's Newbery Medal. It deals with a young boy's struggles with his parents' divorce and being the new kid at school.

MOVIES

Throughout the 1980s, people of all ages went to the movies for entertainment. But watching movies at home became a popular pastime over the course of the decade. This was due to the addition of a new device in many homes called the videocassette recorder (VCR). People rented videotapes from video rental stores and watched films from the comfort of their own home!

In contrast to heavier 1970s movies featuring more controversial topics, 1980s films were generally more lighthearted. *Ghostbusters* and *Beverly Hills Cop* are two representative examples. This was also the decade of the blockbuster. Moviegoers flocked to see films in franchises like Indiana Jones, Star Wars, and Back to the Future.

A LONG RUN!

E.T. the Extra-Terrestrial **holds the record of being the number one movie at the U.S. box office for 16 weeks. It stayed in movie theaters continuously for one year.**

AT THE BOX OFFICE

TOP-GROSSING FILMS OF THE 1980s

- ***E.T. the Extra-Terrestrial*** **(1982)**
- ***Star Wars: Episode V – The Empire Strikes Back*** **(1980)**
- ***Star Wars: Episode VI – Return of the Jedi*** **(1983)**
- ***Indiana Jones and the Last Crusade*** **(1989)**
- ***Batman*** **(1989)**
- ***Raiders of the Lost Ark*** **(1981)**
- ***Back to the Future*** **(1985)**
- ***Top Gun*** **(1986)**
- ***Rain Man*** **(1988)**
- ***Indiana Jones and the Temple of Doom*** **(1984)**

Back to the Future

THE GOONIES

This 1985 adventure movie follows a group of kids who find an ancient pirate's map. The friends go on a quest to find the treasure of "One-Eyed Willy." Bravery and friendship are themes throughout the film, which has gone on to become a classic.

THE PRINCESS BRIDE

The enduring success of *The Princess Bride* may be partly because it has something for all viewers. The film is a mashup of romance, action, and parody. Romantics enjoy the love story between the characters Buttercup and Westley. Adventure fans are captivated by the battles and intrigue in the mythical kingdom of Florin.

GREMLINS

In the quirky 1984 film *Gremlins*, a young man is given a mysterious creature called a mogwai as a Christmas present. When he does not follow the instructions, chaos ensues in the form of many mischievous and murderous Gremlins on the loose. Filmgoers liked the movie's mix of comedy and horror.

THE KARATE KID

Considered by many to be one of the best kids' films of the decade, *The Karate Kid* is a story of personal growth. Daniel LaRusso, a struggling teen, learns to overcome adversity and find happiness by working with karate expert Mr. Miyagi. The film inspired many kids to try martial arts. It also started a franchise of Karate Kid movies.

JOHN HUGHES

American film director John Hughes was known for solidifying the teen movie as its own genre. His coming-of-age stories resonated with young people through their mix of humor, drama, and rebellion. Among his most popular movies are *The Breakfast Club, Pretty in Pink, and Ferris Bueller's Day Off.*

Ferris Bueller's Day Off

TELEVISION AND RADIO

At the start of the 1980s, fewer than one in four American households had cable television. By the end of the decade, more than half of American homes did. Viewers suddenly had many more options for what to watch. VCR technology changed viewing habits by allowing people to record programs and view them at a later time.

Daytime talk shows grew in popularity during the 1980s. At night, sitcoms and dramas dominated programming. Popular family sitcoms included *Family Ties* and *Full House*. Others like *Cheers* and *The Golden Girls* targeted adult audiences. *Hill Street Blues* and *L.A. Law* were well-loved dramas.

Most Americans listened to FM radio stations in the 1980s. Many cities offered listeners FM stations catering to different genres of music. Talk shows on AM stations often targeted listeners of a particular political slant. Rush Limbaugh, a conservative talk show host, saw his political commentary program air nationwide beginning in 1988.

Ted Turner

CNN

On June 1, 1980, broadcasting entrepreneur Ted Turner launched CNN, or Cable News Network. This was the world's first 24-hour news channel. Since its debut, CNN has covered thousands of U.S. and international events. Its live coverage of the Challenger disaster brought much attention to the relatively new network.

VCR

MIAMI VICE

Detectives Sonny Crockett and Ricardo Tubbs solved crimes in this series that debuted in 1984. Its soundtrack, stylish clothes, and scenic backdrop entertained audiences. However, the frequently dark stories often reflected the drug busts common in the news.

THE OPRAH WINFREY SHOW

Oprah Winfrey's daytime talk show began in the mid-1980s. Her relatable interview style, warmth, and compassion for others quickly won over TV audiences. She covered a range of topics from racism to abuse, often sharing personal stories. Her show aired for 25 years. It inspired many others to pursue careers in journalism and media.

MTV

When MTV debuted on August 1, 1981, it changed the music world forever. People could now see videos by their favorite performers 24/7. Video DJs called "veejays" shared the latest music news between videos. MTV altered how artists presented themselves. They needed to look and sound good to sell albums. The network has hugely influenced fashion and pop culture since its start.

THE COSBY SHOW

In 1984, *The Cosby Show* premiered on NBC. The show is sometimes credited with revitalizing the sitcom genre. It was groundbreaking in terms of breaking down racial stereotypes. The show broached topics including teen pregnancy and learning disabilities. It also led to the successful spinoff show *A Different World*, set on a predominantly Black college campus.

MUSIC

Musical genres of the 1980s varied wildly. Rock bands like U2, Bon Jovi, Def Leppard, and Guns N' Roses sold out stadiums in concerts. Pop artists such as Prince were style icons whose lyrics thrilled audiences. The synthesizer was a mainstay in many popular songs and boosted the prominence of the synth-pop genre that had started in the 1970s. MTV made music videos mainstream, helping drive artists like Madonna and Michael Jackson to superstardom.

At the start of the 1980s, people usually bought vinyl LPs or cassette tapes. Compact discs, or CDs, were introduced to the public in 1982. The first CD player for cars, the Pioneer CDX-1, was unveiled in 1984. That same year, the portable CD player, often called the "Discman," came out, too. Sales of CDs grew quickly starting in the mid-1980s. By the decade's end, CD sales had surpassed vinyl LPs.

LIVE AID

On July 13, 1985, a benefit concert called Live Aid was held in London and Philadelphia. Elton John, Phil Collins, Hall and Oates, and Queen were among the performing acts. An estimated 1.9 billion people watched it on TV. The concert raised over $100 million to fight hunger in Ethiopia.

1980s PLAYLIST

- ***Just Can't Get Enough***
  Depeche Mode (1981)
- ***Our Lips Are Sealed***
  The Go-Go's (1981)
- ***Beat It***
  Michael Jackson (1982)
- ***Hungry Like the Wolf***
  Duran Duran (1982)
- ***Born in the U.S.A.***
  Bruce Springsteen (1984)
- ***Jump***
  Van Halen (1984)
- ***Material Girl***
  Madonna (1984)
- ***How Will I Know***
  Whitney Houston (1985)
- ***Planet Rock***
  Afrika Bambaataa and Soulsonic Force (1985)

CD

Depeche Mode

NEW WAVE

Heavily influenced by the punk rock genre of the 1970s, new wave artists created music that was progressive but more pop oriented. Record labels found new wave music more appealing to a wider audience than that of its punk predecessors. Synthesizers were often featured in new wave tracks. Popular artists included the Cure, Culture Club, Depeche Mode, and the Talking Heads.

THRILLER

Michael Jackson released his album *Thriller* in 1982. More than 40 years later, it remains the world's best-selling album of all time. Two of the album's singles, "Billie Jean" and "Beat It," made it to number one on the *Billboard* music chart. Jackson won the Grammy for Album of the Year.

MADONNA

Since her first hit song "Holiday" came out in 1983, Madonna has captivated audiences with her catchy tunes and iconic looks. Her upbeat tempos were popular in dance clubs and heard on radio stations around the globe. Unafraid to push boundaries, Madonna was one of the first celebrities to advocate for awareness on the AIDS epidemic. Her bold rebellion often sparked controversy, too.

BREAK DANCING

Break dancing, or breaking, is a lively dance form. It was created by street dancers in the early hip-hop culture of New York. Break dancers express their creativity and individuality through athletic moves such as head or back spins and fast footwork. Dancers mostly improvise their high-energy, gymnastic moves, which may include stylized steps and poses called freezes.

RAP

Rap exploded in popularity in the 1980s. Many Black and Latino artists used rap to share their experiences and societal frustrations. In 1988, MTV's *Yo! MTV Raps* program debuted. It became an instant hit. Popular 1980s rap artists included Grandmaster Flash, L.L. Cool J, Queen Latifah, and Run-DMC.

Queen Latifah

U.S. SPORTS

When it came to 1980s sports, some teams truly dominated. Between 1980 and 1989, the San Francisco 49ers had the best record of any National Football League (NFL) team. They won the Super Bowl after the 1981, 1984, 1988, and 1989 seasons. Quarterback Joe Montana was a national celebrity. The Edmonton Oilers and the New York Islanders were the superstars of the National Hockey League (NHL). Each won four Stanley Cups during the decade!

The National Basketball Association (NBA) expanded with five new teams. The Dallas Mavericks joined in 1980. The Charlotte Hornets, Miami Heat, Minnesota Timberwolves, and Orlando Magic joined between 1988 and 1989.

MVP

NAME: WAYNE GRETZKY

SPORT: Hockey

YEARS PLAYED: 1979 to 1999

TEAMS: Edmonton Oilers, Los Angeles Kings, St. Louis Blues, New York Rangers

KNOWN FOR: Often called the greatest hockey player of all time, Gretzky won four NHL championships and NHL's Hart Memorial Trophy, an award given to the player deemed most valuable to his team, nine times during the 1980s.

CELTICS
LAKERS

A LEGENDARY RIVALRY

The Boston Celtics and the Los Angeles Lakers were huge NBA rivals throughout the 1980s. The Celtics' Larry Bird and the Lakers' Magic Johnson were two superstars of the decade. But with five NBA Championships to three, the Lakers beat the Celtics for the most titles in the decade.

TENNIS LEGEND

One of the earliest openly gay sports figures, Martina Navratilova is a legend in the tennis world. She won her first U.S. Open in 1983. She was named Player of the Year by the Women's Tennis Association every year from 1982 to 1986.

NASCAR CHAMPIONS

Two dynamite drivers dominated NASCAR in the 1980s. Dale Earnhardt and Darrell Waltrip each won three Cup Series championships and millions of dollars in prize money. Both went on to be inducted into the NASCAR Hall of Fame.

BASEBALL STRIKE OF 1981

Although labor disputes are common in professional sports, the Major League Baseball (MLB) strike in 1981 was a long one. Players went on strike because of disagreements over free-agent compensation. The strike led to 712 MLB regular season games being cancelled between June 12 and August 9. Eventually, team owners and players came to an agreement. But the strike caused an unusual split season.

AEROBICS

Aerobics was one of the biggest physical fitness trends of the 1980s. Aerobics classes often involved catchy music and fun, high-energy dance routines. People liked the motivation of being in a class with others. Actress Jane Fonda revolutionized the fitness craze in April 1982. She released a series of workout videos people could do from home.

GLOBAL SPORTS

Greater women's participation in sports, record-breaking achievements, and new Olympic events were exciting athletic developments in the 1980s. The 1984 Olympic Games was the first to include a women's marathon and the women's road race for cycling. Other sports including synchronized swimming, rhythmic gymnastics, and table tennis also made their Olympic debuts during the decade. Unfortunately, Cold War tensions led to many countries boycotting both the 1980 Olympics in Moscow, Soviet Union, and the 1984 Olympics in Los Angeles, California.

Soccer-loving nations Spain and Mexico hosted the World Cup in the 1980s. West Germany played in the final championship matches of both World Cup events. But the team lost to Italy in 1982 and Argentina in 1986.

OLYMPICS OF THE 1980s

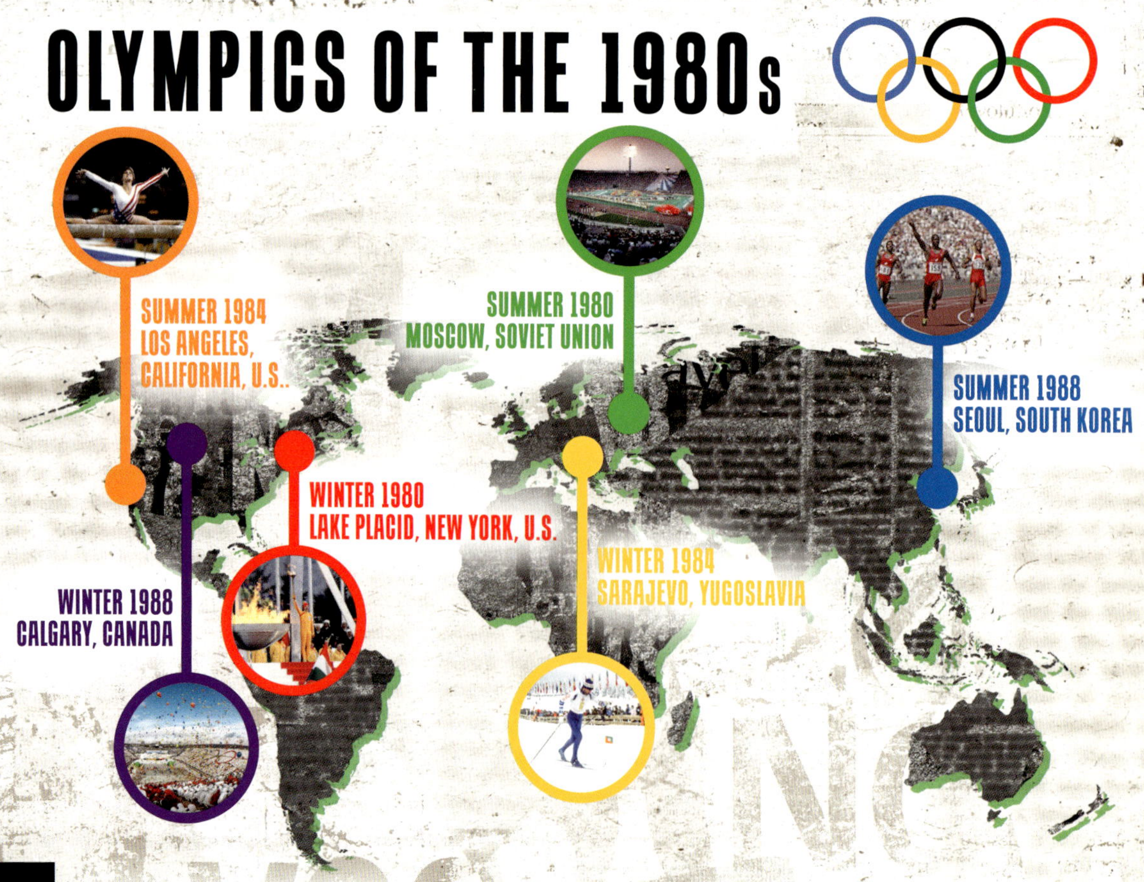

TAKING THE TOUR

Two American cyclists made Tour de France history in the 1980s. In 1984, Marianne Martin won the women's Tour de France bicycle race. She was the first American to win the prestigious race! Greg LeMond became the first American man to win the race in 1986.

MIRACLE ON ICE

On February 22, 1980, the hockey game that became known as the "Miracle on Ice" took place at the Olympic Games in Lake Placid, New York. The Soviet Union's team had won four consecutive Olympic gold medals in hockey. Very much the underdog, the young and inexperienced U.S. team beat the Soviets 4–3. The game remains one of the greatest upsets in sports history.

NEW COMPETITORS

The International Blind Sports Federation (ISBA) was founded in 1981. Since that time, the organization has hosted many athletic competitions. It has also worked to advance opportunities and representation for blind and visually impaired athletes. These athletes now compete around the globe at events such as the Paralympic Games and the ISBA World Games.

LACROSSE CHAMPIONSHIPS

Lacrosse is the oldest team sport in America. The Haudenosaunee, or Iroquois, people played it as far back as 1100 CE. England hosted the first Women's Lacrosse World Cup in 1982. The U.S. team won against Australia in the final game.

1986 WORLD CUP

Two of soccer's most incredible plays occurred when Argentina played England during the quarterfinals of the 1986 World Cup. Argentinian legend Diego Maradona made a goal by punching the ball with a closed fist. This controversial goal became known as the "Hand of God." Just minutes later, Maradona ran lightning-fast through the English defenders and goalkeeper, scoring what was called the "Goal of the Century."

A UNIQUE FEAT

East Germany's Christa Luding-Rothenburger is a singular athlete. She is the only person to ever have won medals in both the Winter and Summer Olympics in the same year. At the 1988 Winter Olympics in Calgary, Canada, she won gold in the 1000m and silver in the 500m speed skating competitions. At the Summer Olympics in Seoul, South Korea, she won the silver medal in the track cycling sprint event.

TIMELINE

FEBRUARY 22, 1980
In what becomes known as the "Miracle on Ice," the U.S. hockey team defeats the Soviet team at the Winter Olympic Games

MAY 18, 1980
Mount Saint Helens erupts in Washington State

MAY 22, 1980
The video game *Pac-Man* makes its debut in an arcade in Tokyo, Japan

JUNE 29, 1980
Vigdis Finnbogadottir becomes the world's first democratically elected woman president, going on to serve as president of Iceland for 16 years

NOVEMBER 4, 1980
Ronald Reagan is elected president of the U.S.

JANUARY 20, 1981
After 444 days in captivity, American hostages in Tehran, Iran, are freed

MARCH 30, 1981
John Hinckley Jr. attempts to assassinate President Reagan

JUNE 5, 1981
Dr. Michael Gottlieb's report, the earliest clinical AIDS description, is published in the CDC newsletter

AUGUST 1, 1981
MTV makes its debut broadcast

JUNE 12, 1982
About one million people protest against nuclear weapons in New York City's Central Park

FEBRUARY 25, 1982
Wisconsin signs into law a bill making it illegal to discriminate against people based on sexual orientation

MARCH 1983
Motorola's DynaTAC 8000X, the world's first commercially available cell phone, goes on sale

JUNE 11, 1982
The sci-fi film *E.T. the Extra-Terrestrial* opens in movie theaters across the U.S.

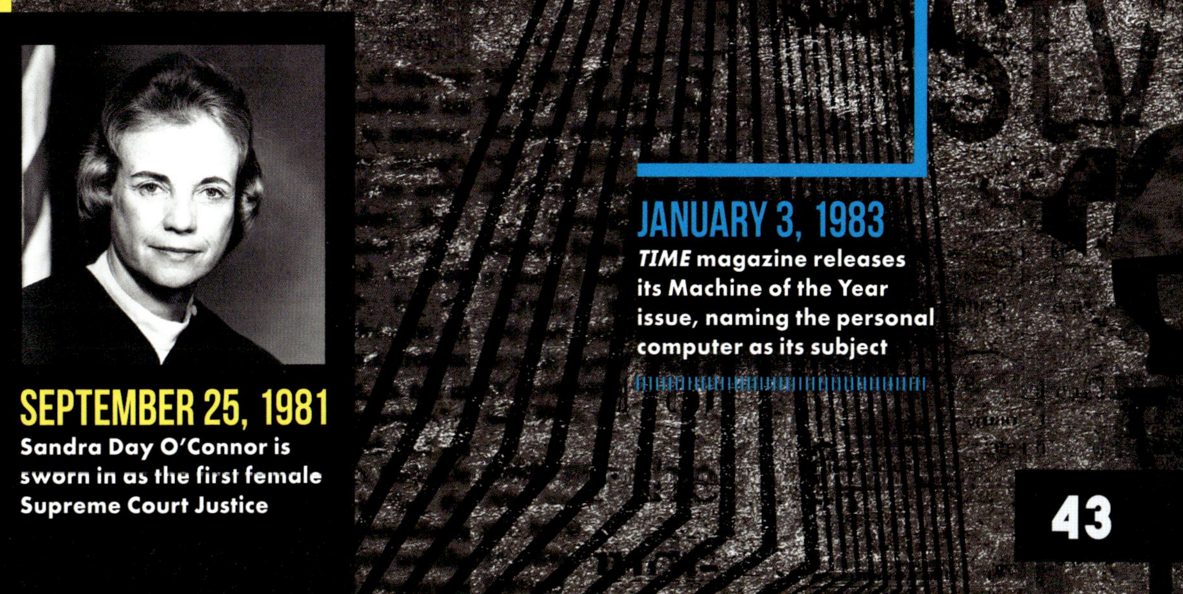

JANUARY 3, 1983
TIME magazine releases its Machine of the Year issue, naming the personal computer as its subject

SEPTEMBER 25, 1981
Sandra Day O'Connor is sworn in as the first female Supreme Court Justice

JANUARY 24, 1984
The Apple Macintosh computer goes on sale

SEPTEMBER 1, 1985
Oceanographer Robert Ballard and his team find the remains of the RMS *Titanic* off the Canadian coast

MAY 1985
Scientists publish the first scholarly paper describing their recent discovery of a hole in Earth's ozone layer

APRIL 26, 1986
An explosion occurs at the nuclear power plant in Chernobyl releasing radiation into the atmosphere

JULY 13, 1985
About 1.9 billion people tune in to the Live Aid benefit concert that takes place in London and Philadelphia

JANUARY 28, 1986
NASA's Space Shuttle Challenger breaks apart shortly after launch, killing all seven crew members

FEBRUARY 28, 1984
Michael Jackson wins a record-breaking eight Grammys

MARCH 19, 1987
The FDA approves the use of AZT, the first anti-HIV medication

OCTOBER 19, 1987

The U.S. stock market crashes, triggering other economic crises around the world

DECEMBER 8, 1987

Ronald Reagan and Mikhail Gorbachev sign the Intermediate-Range Nuclear Forces Treaty, eliminating a class of nuclear weapons

NOVEMBER 8, 1988

Republican candidate George H.W. Bush defeats Democrat Michael Dukakis in the U.S. presidential election

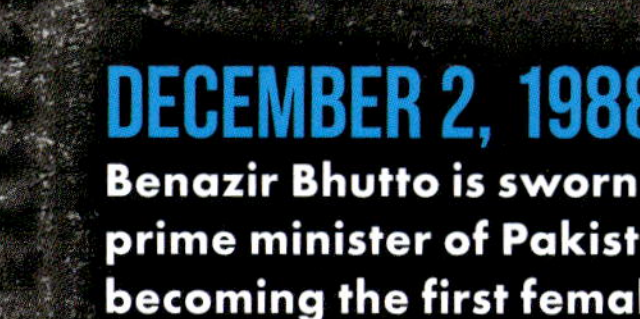

DECEMBER 2, 1988

Benazir Bhutto is sworn in as prime minister of Pakistan, becoming the first female leader of a Muslim country in modern history

JANUARY 22, 1989

The San Francisco 49ers win the Super Bowl for the third time during the decade

MARCH 24, 1989

The *Exxon Valdez* runs aground, dumping 11 million gallons of oil into Alaska's Prince William Sound

NOVEMBER 9, 1989

The Berlin Wall is torn down, marking the first step towards the reunification of Germany

GLOSSARY

adversity—a state of continued difficulty or misfortune

advocacy—related to the act of supporting a cause

animatronic—related to dolls or robots that move through electromechanical devices

climate change—a human-caused change in Earth's weather due to warming temperatures

Cold War—a conflict between the U.S. and the Soviet Union in the second half of the 1900s that did not break out into fighting

communism—a social system in which property and goods are controlled by the government

compensation—payment

conservative—related to traditional values

disarmament—the reduction of weapons or the withdrawal of military forces

discrimination—the act of treating someone unfairly because of race, gender, age, or other differences

disposable income—money that is left after taxes to be used or saved as one wishes

genre—a category of a kind of art based on style, form, or content

gentrified—having undergone a process in which poor areas experience an influx of middle-class or wealthy people that results in an increase of property values and the displacement of earlier, poorer residents

immune system—the body system that protects the body from illness or disease

inflation—a general increase in the prices of goods and a drop in the purchasing power of money

labor unions—organizations of workers who come together to get fair treatment, improve working conditions, and ensure other workers' rights

LGBTQ+—a community of people who identify as something other than heterosexual or the gender they were assigned at birth; LGBTQ+ stands for Lesbian, Gay, Bisexual, Transgender, Queer and other identities.

liberal—related to liberalism; liberalism is the inclination to be open to ideas that are not traditional.

marginalized—relating to people who are treated as unimportant or outside the mainstream of society

maximalism—an aesthetic based on bright colors, bold patterns, and a more-is-more attitude

microprocessors—parts of computers that act like the "brain;" a microprocessor is also called a microchip.

nuclear power plant—a facility that makes electricity by splitting tiny pieces of matter called atoms

ozone layer—a layer of the atmosphere that blocks most of the Sun's ultraviolet radiation from entering Earth's lower atmosphere

racism—the belief that race is a fundamental part of human traits and that certain races are superior to others

radiation—waves of energy sent out by sources of heat or light

Reaganomics—an economic plan put into effect by President Reagan that included cuts to social programs, significant tax cuts, and increased military spending

Soviet—related to the Soviet Union; short for the Union of Soviet Socialist Republics, the Soviet Union is a former country in Eastern Europe and western Asia made up of 15 republics or states that broke up in 1991.

stigma—a set of negative or unfair beliefs that a society or group of people have about something

WRITE ABOUT IT!

- What do you think were the most important moments during the 1980s? **Why?**
- Which part of the 1980s would you have liked to experience? **Why?**
- Are there any events from the 1980s that you think affect life today?

INDEX

The images in this book are reproduced through the courtesy of: Science History Images/ Alamy Stock Photo, front cover (Sandra Day O'Connor); Razulation, front cover (phone); Fred Jewell/ AP Images, front cover (Wayne Gretzky), p. 39 (strike); ASSOCIATED PRESS/ AP Images, front cover (NBA), p. 41 (miracle); CBW/ Alamy Stock Photo, front cover (book); Allstar Picture Library Ltd/ Alamy Stock Photo, front cover (The Goonies); Pictorial Press Ltd/ Alamy Stock Photo, front cover (Live Aid); ClassicStock/ Getty Images, pp. 3 (Mount Saint Helens), 5 (listening), 9 (Mount Saint Helens), 27 (suits); Harry Langdon/ Getty Images, pp. 3 (Jane Fonda), 39 (Jane Fonda); Peter Turnley/ Getty Images, pp. 3 (Punk Fashion), 27 (Punk Fashion); Shawshots/ Alamy Stock Photo, pp. 3 (E.T.), 32 (E.T.); Namco/ Wikipedia, pp. 4 (Pac-Man), 42 (Pac-Man); adsR/ Alamy Stock Photo, p. 4 (Hamburger Helper); Chris Willson/ Alamy Stock Photo, p. 4 (Atari 2600); xMarshall, p. 4 (Reeboks); INTERFOTO/ Alamy Stock Photo, p. 5; Jack Thornell/ AP Images, p. 6; Winai Tepsuttinun, p. 7 (gas); Photo Builder, p. 7 (newspaper); tab62, p. 7 (eggs); phive2015, p. 7 (bread); Hajrudin, p. 7 (Hershey's Bar); Dirck Halstead/ Getty Images, p. 8 (Reagan); Diana Walker/ Getty Images, p. 8 (Iran-Contra); Leif Skoogfors/ Getty Images, p. 8 (protest); Anchorage Daily News/ Getty Images, p. 9 (Exxon Valdez); Colin McConnell/ Getty Images, p. 9 (banner); White House Photo/ Wikipedia, p. 10; The U.S. National Archives/ Wikipedia, p. 11 (O'Connor); wilsonbrad89/ Wikipedia, p. 11 (Ferrarro); Images Press/ Getty Images, p. 11 (protest); Science & Society Picture Library/ Getty Images, p. 12; Brian Vander Brug/ Getty Images, p. 13 (Gottlieb); Art Zelin/ Getty Images, p. 13 (Hudson); Express/ Getty Images, p. 14 (hostages); Ian Cook/ Getty Images, p. 14 (Gorbachev); Bettmann/ Getty Images, pp. 14 (Belize), 19 (protest), 22 (DeVires), 24 (arcade), 29 (dolls), 40 (winter 1980), 42 (Reagan); Anwar Hussein/ Getty Images, p. 15 (wedding); Langevin Jacques/ Getty Images, p. 15 (Tiananmen Square); Stephen Jaffe/ Getty Images, p. 15 (wall); Wojtek Laski/ Getty Images, p. 16; Chuck Nacke/ Alamy Stock Photo, p. 17; Harold M. Lambert/ Getty Images, pp. 18-19; Chip HIRES/ Getty Images, p. 19 (Bhutto); David Turnley/ Getty Images, p. 19 (marriage); Robert R. McElroy/ Getty Images, p. 19 (Graham); Photology1971, p. 20; StudioEdo/ Flickr, p. 21 (TIME); Bob Riha Jr/ Getty Images, pp. 21 (camcorder), 44 (MJ); NASA/ Wikipedia, pp. 22 (Ride), 23; NOAA/ IFE/ URI/ Wikipedia, p. 22 (Titanic); HUM Images/ Getty Images, p. 24 (Minivan); PixieMe, p. 24 (EPCOT); Michael Ochs Archives/ Getty Images, pp. 26, 33 (The Goonies), 37 (dancing); Museum Rotterdam/ Wikipedia, p. 27 (shoes); Photo 12/ Alamy Stock Photo, p. 27 (mullet); D Graphics, p. 28 (Rubiks); Dennis Hallinan/ Getty Images, p. 28 (Pac-Man); Andrew Gardner/ Alamy Stock Photo, p. 28 (board game); Evan-Amos/ Wikipedia, p. 29 (ball); MelissaMN, p. 29 (puppies); Earl Kenneth/ Wikipedia, p. 29 (teddy); Christina Leaf, p. 30; Ben__Stevens, p. 31 (adventure); Theo Wargo/ Getty Images, p. 31 (Van Allsburg); SpiraSoph/ Wikipedia, p. 31 (Cleary); Allstar Picture Library Limited./ Alamy Stock Photo, pp. 32, 33 (The Princess Bride, Ferris Bueller), 37 (Thriller); Sunset Boulevard/ Getty Images, p. 33 (Gremlins); Rick Diamond/ Getty Images, p. 34 (CNN); LIAL, p. 34 (VCR); Silver Screen Collection/ Getty Images, p. 35 (Miami Vice); Afro Newspaper/ Gado/ Getty Images, p. 35 (Oprah); Album/ Alamy Stock Photo, p. 35 (Cosby); Dave Hogan/ Getty Images, p. 36 (Live Aid); nuruddean, p. 36 (CD); Koh Hasebe/ Shinko Music/ Getty Images, p. 37 (new wave); Raymond Boyd/ Getty Images, p. 37 (rapping); B Bennett/ Getty Images, p. 38; Boston Celtics/ Wikipedia, p. 39 (Celtics); Los Angeles Lakers/ Wikipedia, p. 39 (Lakers); Steve Powell/ Getty Images, p. 39 (tennis); Bob Thomas/ Getty Images, p. 40 (summer 1984); Gilbert Iundt Jean-Yves Ruszniewski/ Getty Images, p. 40 (winter 1988, summer 1980); David Madison/ Getty Images, p. 40 (winter 1984); Mike Powell/ Getty Images, p. 40 (summer 1988); Gocal83/ Wikipedia, p. 41 (LeMond); Estadio/ Wikipedia, p. 41 (World Cup); Ketsarinya, p. 41 (lacrosse); Henry Zbyszynski/ Wikipedia, p. 42 (1980); CillBill - Loyalkaspar/ Wikipedia, p. 43 (MTV); Jessyy, p. 43 (O'Connor); Barbara Alper/ Getty Images, p. 43 (1982); Redrum0486/ Wikipedia, p. 43 (phone); Alpha Historica/ Alamy Stock Photo, p. 44 (1984); Luckyicons, p. 44 (gas mask); ZUMA Press, Inc./ Alamy Stock Photo, p. 45 (1989); CHRIS WILKINS/ Getty Images, p. 45 (Exxon Valdez).